I0002742

CONTENTS

Illustrations

Introduction

America is under widespread attack in cyberspace. Unlike in air, land, and sea domains, we lack dominance in cyberspace and could grow increasingly vulnerable if we do not fundamentally change how we view this battlespace.

--General James E. Cartwright

Is the United States Air Force prepared to survive a cyber attack? The service "flies" in cyberspace every day and faces multiple threats during each flight. Air Force missions, both critical and non-critical, are becoming more dependent upon cyberspace with each passing day. The service maintains a vigilant cyber defense but is it resilient enough to survive a cyber attack and continue operating in a contested cyber domain?

This paper investigates the Air Force's defense of cyberspace in preparation for a cyber attack. It reviews national and military cyber strategy and doctrine to reveal the Air Force's outlook on cyber defense. This outlook characterizes the balance established between offensive and defensive cyber operations. This paper proposes that the view that "air power is primarily an offensive weapon"[1] influences the Air Force's approach toward offensive cyber operations. An unbalanced approach favoring offensive cyber operations may make the Air Force less prepared for a cyber attack.

A thorough understanding of military defense theory establishes a framework to comprehend defense of the cyber domain. Carl Von Clausewitz offers a comprehensive theory of defense relevant to all

---

[1] Colonel Phillip Melinger, USAF, *10 Propositions Regarding Air Power.* (Air Force History and Museums Program, 1995), 14.

domains including cyber. An examination of Clausewitz's theory of defense, in chapter 3, provides a useable construct for the defense of cyberspace. Clausewitz's theory of defense is used to evaluate the Air Force's current cyber defense posture to determine its susceptibility to attack.

Adversaries have not yet tested the service's cyber defenses to a major cyber attack, but other nations have been attacked and survived. Estonia endured a cyber attack in 2007 that disrupted and severely tested its defense. This thesis examines the Estonian case to inform Air Force preparations for defending and surviving cyber attacks.

The current Air Force cyber defense posture, Clausewitz's theory of defense, and the example of Estonia are used to offer recommendations for a more complete Air Force defense in the cyber domain. The information gleaned from these areas provides actions the Air Force can take to prepare for a cyber attack. Chapter 2 reviews US strategy and doctrine to determine the balance between cyber attack and defense operations. Chapter 3 discusses Clausewitz's theory of defense and its applicability in the cyber domain. Estonia's actions in the first web war are analyzed in Chapter 4 to identify effective cyber defense practices. The remainder of this chapter sets the stage for the following chapters by describing the current cyberspace environment in which the Air Force operates.

The Cyberspace Environment

The *US National Military Strategy for Cyberspace Operations* defines cyberspace as "a domain characterized by the use of electronics and the electromagnetic spectrum to store, modify, and exchange data via networked systems and associated physical infrastructures."[2] This definition captures the vastness of the cyber domain. Cyberspace

---

[2] Department of Defense, *The National Military Strategy for Cyberspace Operations, December 2006* (Washington DC: Department of Defense, 2006), ix, http://www.dod mil/pubs/foi/ojcs/07-F-2105doc1.pdf. Document in now declassified.

includes the electrons, the data, the software, and the physical machines in cyberspace. This domain is large, complex and changes every day.

The United States depends on freedom of action in cyberspace. America's "economy and national security are fully dependent upon information technology and the information infrastructure."[3] An estimated 200 million Americans connect to the Internet at home or work.[4] As much as 25 percent of the US economy traverses through the cyber domain every day.[5] A cyber attack that denies America's access to cyberspace will cripple business and government operations.

Cyberspace is a dynamic environment. Changes occur as systems are added and removed from the domain. Cyberspace becomes more complex over time in the types and amounts of hardware and software used to access and operate in cyberspace.

Computing hardware continues to advance with faster and more capable microprocessors. "The original Apple II computer of 1977 used an eight-bit processor that ran at one megahertz. The PC standard today is a 64-bit chip running at 3.6 gigahertz--effectively, 28,800 times as fast."[6] Advanced hardware with faster processing speeds demonstrates how the cyber environment becomes more complex over time and why it requires sophisticated methods of operations.

Advanced hardware allows for the development of more complex software. Software developers, like Microsoft, add more functions to products to utilize faster processing speeds. Microsoft is a leading software manufacturer for PC computers. They produce the Windows brand operating system that provides a user-friendly interface for computers. The latest member of the Windows family of operating

---

[3] *The National Strategy to Secure Cyberspace, February 2003* (Washington DC: White House, 2003), viii.
[4] US House, *Cybersecurity: A Review of Public and Private Efforts to Secure Our Nation's Internet Infrastructure: Hearing before the Subcommittee on Information Policy, Census, and National Archives of the Committee on Oversight and Government Reform,* 110th Cong., 1st sess., 23 October 2007, 7.
[5] US House, *Cybersecurity,* 23 Oct 2007, 78.
[6] Robert X. Cringley, "Parallel Universe," *Technology Review,* January/February 2009, http://www.technologyreview.com/alt-thinking/hp_feature_article.aspx?id=21806&pg=1.

systems is Vista. This software runs on 50 million lines of code.[7]
Microsoft's Windows 95, an early member of the Windows family, was
released in 1995 and ran 15 million lines of code.[8] In the span of
fourteen years, the number of lines of software code more than tripled.
Increases expand the capability of software and allow it to keep pace with
user demands for more functionality, and it also makes the product more
complex to manage.

Software complexity has a direct bearing on computer security.
"Unfortunately, complexity is bad for security. It creates more places for
bugs to lurk, makes interactions among software components harder to
understand, and increases the flow rate of packets well past where
anyone can easily reconstruct what happened when things go wrong."[9]
The Air Force will have difficulty defending cyberspace as computer
hardware and software become more complex.

Many vulnerabilities exist in cyberspace as a result of the
increased complexity of the environment. The Computer Security
Institute produces an annual Computer Crime & Security Survey that
lists the key types of computer security incidents among survey
participants. In 1999, the top two types of incidents were viruses and
insider abuse.[10] In 2008, viruses and insider abuse remained at the top
but the complexity of the environment led to the emergence of a new
threat, botnets[11] (an explanation of botnets is provided later in this
chapter). Georgia Tech also cited botnets, along with malware, as two of
the top five emerging computer threats for 2009.[12] These two threats,

[7] Steve Lohr and John Markoff, "Windows Is So Slow, but Why?," *New York Times*, 27 March 2006, http://www nytimes.com/2006/03/27/technology/27soft html?_r=2&pagewanted=all (accessed 12 April 2009).
[8] Steve Lohr and John Markoff, "Windows Is So Slow, but Why?," *New York Times*, 27 March 2006, http://www nytimes.com/2006/03/27/technology/27soft html?_r=2&pagewanted=all (accessed 12 April 2009).
[9] Martin C. Libicki, *Conquest in Cyberspace: National Security and Information Warfare* (Cambridge, NY: Cambridge University Press, 2007), 293.
[10] Robert Richardson, *2008 CSI Computer Crime & Security Survey*, Computer Security Institute (New York, NY: CSI, 2008), 15.
[11] Robert Richardson, *2008 CSI Computer Crime & Security Survey*, 2008, 15.
[12] Georgia Tech Information Security Center, *Emerging Cyber Threats Report for 2009* (Atlanta, GA: GTISC, 15 October 2008), 1.

malware and botnets, indicate the increasing complexity of threats in cyberspace.

Malware is a broad term that describes any malicious software created to damage a computer system.[13] Malware creators have developed more sophisticated delivery methods for their expanding line of products in recent times. Kaspersky Lab, a computer protection company, reportedly discovered 28,940 different malware programs on users' computers in August 2008, which was an increase of over 8,000 from the previous month.[14]

Malware threats are increasing because their distributors are becoming better at deceiving naïve computer users into downloading malicious code.[15] For example, unsuspecting users receive an apparently innocent e-mail with a link to a seemingly legitimate website. Users may be prompted to download a software update to view the site they were attempting to access. This download, however, may install malware rather than the innocent update advertised. The unsuspecting user therefore infects his computer and may not notice any difference in its operations.[16]

Malware infection may be the first step in the recruitment and formation of botnets. Botnets are a concentration of malware-infected computers remotely controlled by one individual, called a botherder. The botherder can direct his army of botnets for various types of malicious activity such as data theft, denial of service attacks (DoS), and spam delivery.[17] Botherders harness the computing power and bandwidth of large numbers of bot clients. "A small botnet of 10,000 bot clients with, conservatively, 128Kbps broadband upload speed can produce approximately 1.3 gigabits of data per second...probably powerful enough

---

[13] Air Force Doctrine Document (AFDD) 2-11 (Draft), *Cyberspace Operations*, 24 October 2008, 59.
[14] GTISC, *Emerging Cyber Threats Report for 2009*, 1.
[15] GTISC, *Emerging Cyber Threats Report for 2009*, 1.
[16] GTISC, *Emerging Cyber Threats Report for 2009*, 1.
[17] GTISC, *Emerging Cyber Threats Report for 2009*, 2.

to take down most of the Fortune 500 companies."[18] This is not just a theoretical problem. The Georgia Tech report cited a Panda Labs report in which "10 million bot computers were used to distribute spam and malware across the Internet each day."[19]

Cyberspace Adversaries

There are several different types of adversaries employing threats in cyberspace. Air Force General Kevin Chilton, Commander, USSTRATCOM, provided an apt description of the different types of adversaries found in cyberspace during his 17 March 2009 testimony before the House Armed Services Committee. "The threats...kind of span from what I'll call the bored teenager, which was really kind of maybe the first threats we started seeing in the hacker world back in the 1990s, through, obviously, much more sophisticated threats that we're seeing, criminal activity out there, all the way up to threats that could be sponsored by...nation-states that could potentially threaten not only our military networks but also our critical national networks."[20] General Chilton's characterization of adversaries demonstrates three distinct threats: the bored teenager hacker, the criminal hacker, and the nation-state.[21]

The bored teenager hacker is often pictured as a young adult seeking the thrill derived from hacking into computer systems and displaying their mastery of technology. This type of hacker is similar to automobile joy riders. A joy rider typically steals a car for the sheer thrill of the adventure and then abandons the vehicle when the thrill is over. The bored teenager hacker may hack into a computer system for the fun of breaking through the defenses but will do little damage other than

---

[18] Craig A. Schiller et al., *Botnets: The Killer Web App* (St. Louis, MO: Syngress, 2007), 5-6.

[19] GTISC, *Emerging Cyber Threats Report for 2009*, 2.

[20] House, *On The United States Strategic Command: Hearing before the Strategic Forces Subcommitte of the House Committee on Armed Services*, 111th Cong., 17 March 2009.

[21] House, *On The United States Strategic Command: Hearing before the Strategic Forces Subcommitte of the House Committee on Armed Services*, 111th Cong., 17 March 2009.

perhaps leaving computer graffiti as evidence of his activity.[22] The Air Force will always have to cope with individual hackers in cyberspace, but these adversaries will be more of a menace than an overt threat to military systems.

Crackers, individuals hacking for criminal purposes,[23] increasingly threaten the cyberspace environment. Experts project "that cyber crime will become increasingly organized and profit-driven in the years ahead."[24] Criminals have organized themselves in the cyber domain to take advantage of the large profits made from illegal computer activity such as credit card and identity theft. The Air Force maintains sensitive personnel data in cyberspace and must be vigilant in defending this data against crackers.

Crackers also contribute to the proliferation of threats by selling the tools they use for illegal activity to any individual willing to pay. "You can buy, lease, subscribe and even pay-as-you-go to obtain the latest malware kits, which are much more sophisticated than their predecessors."[25] The selling of criminal tools is "managed [by] service providers that wrap new services around malware kits to increase propagation and enable organized fraud on a global scale."[26] The creation and selling of criminal tools ensures a ready supply of threats for the Air Force to defend against in cyberspace.

The last group of adversaries identified in General Chilton's testimony is the nation-state. This group might prove to be the most threatening to the US Air Force. A nation-state can add cyber capabilities to its arsenal for a low cost that could cause widespread disruptions to private and public business in the United States. China

---

[22] Winn Schwartau, *CyberShock: Surviving Hackers, Phreakers, Identity Thieves, Internet Terrorists and Weapons of Mass Disruption* (New York, NY: Thunder's Mouth Press, 2000), 25.

[23] Winn Schwartau, *CyberShock: Surviving Hackers, Phreakers, Identity Thieves, Internet Terrorists and Weapons of Mass Disruption* (New York, NY: Thunder's Mouth Press, 2000), 41.

[24] GTISC, *Emerging Cyber Threats Report for 2009*, 6.

[25] GTISC, *Emerging Cyber Threats Report for 2009*, 6.

[26] GTISC, *Emerging Cyber Threats Report for 2009*, 6.

exemplifies the rise of computer operations by a nation-state as it continues to increase its capability in cyber operations by "establish[ing] information warfare units to develop viruses to attack enemy computer systems and networks."[27]

The recently released 2009 Department of Defense (DoD) report to Congress on the military power of China contains numerous references to China's expanding operations in cyberspace. "PRC [People's Republic of China] military writings highlight the seizure of electromagnetic dominance in the early phases of a campaign as among the foremost tasks to ensure battlefield success."[28] China is also investing resources into cyber operations including the creation of military units to carry out computer network attack (CNA), computer network exploitation (CNE), and computer network defense (CND).[29] These are threats the Air Force will likely face in any military action with China.

Nation-state actors are using hackers to spy on other nations. Recent news stories describe a spy network based in China called GhostNet. This network "has hacked into computer networks around the world, stealing classified information from governments and private organisations in more than 100 countries."[30] "A spokesman for the Chinese Consulate in New York dismissed the idea that China was involved."[31]

Nation states also seek the use of cyberspace to gain a possible advantage in the case of conflict. United States officials reported that China and Russia hacked into the US power grid and installed malware

---

[27] Department of Defense, *Annual Report to Congress: Military Power of the People's Republic of China 2009* (Washington, DC: Office of the Secretary of Defense, 2009), 27-28.
[28] Department of Defense, *Annual Report to Congress: Military Power of the People's Republic of China 2009* (Washington, DC: Office of the Secretary of Defense, 2009), 14.
[29] Department of Defense, *Annual Report to Congress: Military Power of the People's Republic of China 2009*, 27.
[30] Aljazeera, "Global 'Cyber Spy' Network Revealed," *Aljazerra.net*, 30 March 2009, http://english.aljazeera net/news/americas/2009/03/20093303304496652 html.
[31] John Markoff, "Vast Spy System Loots Computers in 103 Countries," New York Times, 28 March 2009, http://www nytimes.com/2009/03/29/technology/29spy html?_r=1&scp=1&sq=ghost%20net&st=cse (accessed 4 June 2009).

capable of causing massive power disruptions.[32] No damage was discovered but it was feared that the malware could be activated at will and cause much damage in the event of a crisis.[33] These recent news items display the increased activity and sophistication of the nation state adversary.

Air Force Dependence on Cyberspace

The Air Force depends on cyberspace to execute routine mission functions. Service members currently perform many personnel actions via cyberspace instead of through a base-level personnel office, thereby saving the Air Force manpower while maintaining the quality of service. The service uses cyberspace for routine mission functions like military relocations (PCSs) and promotions.

The Air Force created the virtual military personnel flight (vMPF) as a tool for members' use to accomplish many actions on-line instead of physically reporting to the MPF. The brick and mortar MPF is the location where administrative personnel actions occur in the Air Force. In the past, a member would visit the MPF to start the relocation process from one base to another. The member was required to receive an initial assignment briefing from an MPF representative to start the relocation process. Various paper work was also physically submitted to and received from the MPF requiring multiple visits by the member. Personnel can now accomplish these same actions from their office using vMPF.

The vMPF also helps military members perform other routine functions in addition to relocations. Air Force personnel can review duty information like decorations and performance reports using vMPF. The Air Force stores service members' performance reports at the Air Force Personnel Center in Texas. In the past, members had to travel there to

---

[32] Siobhan Gorman, "Electricity Grid in U.S. Penetrated By Spies," *The Wall Street Journal*, 8 April 2009, http://online.wsj.com/article/SB123914805204099085 html (accessed 12 April 2009).
[33] Siobhan Gorman, "Electricity Grid in U.S. Penetrated By Spies," *The Wall Street Journal*, 8 April 2009.

view paper copies of their official records. Today, they can request and receive electronic copies of their records via e-mail. The vMPF relies on the cyber domain to perform its many functions.

The Air Force also relies on cyberspace for mission critical operations. The Air and Space Operations Center (AOC) offers a good example of a facility that depends on cyberspace to conduct many mission-critical operations. The AOC "provides operational-level C2 [command and control] of air and space forces as the focal point for planning, directing, and assessing air and space operations."[34] The AOC produces the Air Tasking Order (ATO) that organizes the daily air operations. The AOC relies on connectivity through the cyber domain to perform its mission.

The AOC is composed of numerous computer systems designed to perform the functions of the various AOC divisions. Hundreds of computer terminals link systems within the AOC to other AOC systems as well as to systems outside the AOC. The ATO is distributed electronically using network connections to all units requiring a copy. The Air Force relies on freedom of action in cyberspace to maintain AOC operations.

The vMPF and AOC examples highlight how the Air Force depends on cyberspace for both routine and mission-critical operations and functions. The Air Force continues to expand its operations in cyberspace as it looks for ways to perform existing missions with limited resources. Defense of cyberspace is critical as the Air Force migrates more functions and missions to the cyber domain.

Summary

This brief look at the current cyber environment, cyber adversaries, and dependence on cyberspace sets the stage for the

---

[34] Air Force Instruction (AFI) 113-1 AOC V3, *Operational Procedures—Air and Space Operations Center*, 1 August 2005, 9.

discussion of the Air Force's defense of cyberspace. The cyber domain is a complex environment that contains sophisticated threats. Malware and botnets are two threats developed to harness computer power for malicious activity in cyberspace. Botnets have the potential of massing myriads of unsuspecting computers in attacks against corporations or governments.

The adversaries found in cyberspace have also become more sophisticated. Criminals are using the cyber domain for illicit profit and becoming more organized in their activities. Nation-states, like China, continue to emphasize cyberspace as an area of future conflict that the Air Force must defend against.

The Air Force depends on the cyber domain to perform both non-critical and critical mission functions. The service continues to emphasize the use of cyberspace to perform business. Freedom of action in cyberspace is required for the Air Force to conduct future operations effectively. The Air Force requires a sophisticated cyber defense to thwart possible attackers

Is the Air Force prepared to defend itself in the face of such a hostile environment? The next chapter examines the posture of the Air Force for cyber operations as found in its doctrine and other writings. This review will highlight the position the Air Force is taking to defend itself in cyberspace.

Chapter 1

The Air Force View of Defense in Cyberspace

At the very heart of warfare lies doctrine. It represents the central beliefs for waging war in order to achieve victory. Doctrine is of the mind, a network of faith and knowledge reinforced by experience which lays the pattern for the utilization of men, equipment, and tactics. It is the building material for strategy. It is fundamental to sound judgment.

-- *General Curtis E. LeMay*

How has the Air Force positioned itself to defend against a cyber attack? The answer to this question is found in the service's doctrine. This chapter traces cyberspace strategy from the national level down to the Air Force and describes how the service has interpreted cyberspace strategy in preparation for operating and defending this domain.

It is difficult to trace cyberspace strategy to Air Force doctrine because many documents about the cyber domain are classified. The United States government has recently become more transparent regarding the cyber domain so that it can defend public and private interests against the rising number of attacks in cyberspace. The Bush administration released the *National Strategy to Secure Cyberspace* in February 2003 as "a framework for protecting this infrastructure that is essential to our economy, security, and way of life."[1]

National Cyber Strategy

The *National Strategy to Secure Cyberspace* identifies three strategic objectives: "Prevent cyber attacks against America's critical infrastructures; Reduce national vulnerability to cyber attacks; and Minimize damage and recovery time from cyber attacks that do occur."[2]

---

[1] *The National Strategy to Secure Cyberspace, February 2003* (Washington DC: White House, 2003), iii.
[2] *The National Strategy to Secure Cyberspace, February 2003*, viii.

These three objectives focus on the defense of the cyber domain from the point of preventing attacks to recovering from attacks after they occur.

The strategy identified five national priorities to achieve the three strategic objectives:

I. A National Cyberspace Security Response System
II. A National Cyberspace Security Threat and Vulnerability Reduction Program
III. A National Cyberspace Security Awareness and Training Program
IV. Securing Governments' Cyberspace
V. National Security and International Cyberspace Security Cooperation.[3]

These priorities highlight the strategy's emphasis on reducing the vulnerability to attacks, responding to cyber attacks, and preventing future attacks.

Priority I stressed the need for systems to recover from attacks. "No cybersecurity plan can be impervious to concerted and intelligent attacks, information systems must be able to operate while under attack and also have the resilience to restore full operations in their wake...America needs a national cyber disaster recovery plan."[4] This statement reveals that the federal government believes it cannot defend its information systems against all attacks and therefore it must prepare to operate through an attack to the point of fully restoring the information system.

Another theme in the *National Strategy to Secure Cyberspace* is that the government and civilian institutions need to cooperate. The document recognized that the cyber domain is global and spans governments, commercial industries, and private citizens. Defending against this global threat "requires a system of international cooperation to enable the information sharing, reduce vulnerabilities, and deter

---

[3] *The National Strategy to Secure Cyberspace, February 2003*, x.
[4] *The National Strategy to Secure Cyberspace, February 2003*, 3.

malicious actors"[5] to defend the cyber domain properly. "Without such cooperation, our collective ability to detect, deter, and minimize the effects of cyber-based attacks would be greatly diminished."[6]

The strategy identified actions US organizations need to perform in preparation for cyber attacks. Two of the identified actions, contingency planning and counterattack, are especially relevant to the US military. "Contingency planning is a key element of cybersecurity."[7] The US government needs contingency plans to handle disruptions and to ensure continuity of operations.[8] After surviving an initial cyber attack, the United States must be prepared to counterattack. Regarding a cyber attack on the United States, the strategy announced that "the United States reserves the right to respond in an appropriate manner. The United States will be prepared for such contingencies."[9]

The *National Strategy to Secure Cyberspace* initiated a strategy for securing cyberspace at the national level. It recognized the vulnerabilities the United States faces in this domain and the need for both public and private sectors to share in the defense of cyberspace. The call for defense covered the early detection of threats and extended through the recovery of systems targeted in an attack. This strategy emphasized the need to recover from and continue operations through a cyber attack. These broad functional defensive responsibilities should carry-over to the national military strategy for cyber operations.

National Military Cyber Strategy

While the *National Strategy to Secure Cyberspace* focused on defending cyberspace, the *National Military Strategy for Cyberspace Operations* (NMS-CO), December 2006, took a more offensive perspective. Donald Rumsfield, the secretary of defense (SECDEF), at the time of the

---

[5] *The National Strategy to Secure Cyberspace, February 2003*, 4.
[6] *The National Strategy to Secure Cyberspace, February 2003*, 8.
[7] *The National Strategy to Secure Cyberspace, February 2003*, 23.
[8] *The National Strategy to Secure Cyberspace, February 2003*, 23.
[9] *The National Strategy to Secure Cyberspace, February 2003*, 50.

release of the document, set the tone for NMS-CO in the forward where he wrote, "the National Military Strategy for Cyberspace Operations is an important first step toward ensuring our own freedom of action in this contested domain while denying the same to our adversaries."[10] General Peter Pace, the Chairman of the Joint Chiefs of Staff (CJCS) who signed the strategy, echoed the document's offensive tone with the following introductory remarks, "the NMS-CO is the US Armed Forces' comprehensive strategic approach for using cyberspace operations to assure US military strategic superiority in the domain."[11] Strategic superiority in cyberspace is a central theme found in the NMS-CO.

NMS-CO identified three components of computer network operations (CNO): computer network attack (CNA); computer network defense (CND); and computer network exploitation (CNE).[12] CNA is "operations to disrupt, deny, degrade, or destroy"[13] enemy information systems. CND is "actions taken to protect, monitor, analyze, detect, and respond"[14] to actions taken against DoD information systems. CNE are "enabling operations and intelligence collection to gather data from target or adversary automated information systems or networks."[15] CNE is analogous to an air traffic controller. The controller may be supporting either the offensive side in orchestrating an attack or the defensive side by repelling an attack. The classification depends on the context of the activity. CNA is the offensive side of CNO, CND is the defensive side, and CNE could be either offensive or defensive depending on what it is

---

[10] Department of Defense, *The National Military Strategy for Cyberspace Operations, December 2006* (Washington DC: Department of Defense, 2006), v, http://www.dod.mil/pubs/foi/ojcs/07-F-2105doc1.pdf. Document in now declassified.

[11] Department of Defense, *The National Military Strategy for Cyberspace Operations, December 2006*, vi.

[12] Department of Defense, *The National Military Strategy for Cyberspace Operations, December 2006*, GL-1.

[13] Department of Defense, *The National Military Strategy for Cyberspace Operations, December 2006*, GL-1.

[14] Department of Defense, *The National Military Strategy for Cyberspace Operations, December 2006*, GL-1.

[15] Department of Defense, *The National Military Strategy for Cyberspace Operations, December 2006*, GL-1.

enabling. The military strategic goal of NMS-CO is *to ensure US military strategic superiority in cyberspace.*[16] [emphasis in original]

The document listed four strategic priorities to achieve the strategic goal of superiority in cyberspace. Three of the four priorities dealt primarily with offensive operations while one focused on defensive operations. The first priority was to "gain and maintain the initiative to operate within adversary decision cycles."[17] This involves both offense and defense but primarily focuses on using adversary vulnerabilities for offensive operations. The second strategic priority was to integrate cyberspace capabilities into military operations.[18] This means CNO should be included in military plans and future military operations should consider them. The third priority, "build capacity for cyberspace operations,"[19] augments the second priority. The military services need to organize, train, and equip for future CNO. The fourth strategic priority was to "manage risk to cyberspace operations."[20] This deals with threats and vulnerabilities present in the cyber domain and the risk they pose to military operations. The last priority is the most defensive since CND involves indentifying threats and mitigating vulnerabilities.

According to the NMS-CO, cyberspace superiority will "ensure our freedom of action and deny the same for our adversaries."[21] The strategy envisioned several types of cyberspace missions including "setting conditions in cyberspace to ensure the availability of the domain; the ability to engage adversaries decisively to establish cyberspace control and superiority; and the ability to conduct cyberspace operations to achieve desired effects."[22] This mission listing shows the offensive mindset the military has adopted for cyberspace operations.

---

[16] Department of Defense, *The National Military Strategy for Cyberspace Operations, December 2006*, 13.
[17] Department of Defense, *The National Military Strategy for Cyberspace Operations, December 2006*, 19.
[18] Department of Defense, *The National Military Strategy for Cyberspace Operations, December 2006*, 19.
[19] Department of Defense, *The National Military Strategy for Cyberspace Operations, December 2006*, 20.
[20] Department of Defense, *The National Military Strategy for Cyberspace Operations, December 2006*, 20.
[21] Department of Defense, *The National Military Strategy for Cyberspace Operations, December 2006*, 1.
[22] Department of Defense, *The National Military Strategy for Cyberspace Operations, December 2006*, 5.

The NMS-CO tends to emphasize offensive priorities and missions for CNO but the strategy also mentions the defensive side. The "ability to operate through degradation"[23] is listed as a strategic imperative in computer operations. "Elements of this imperative include domain resilience, redundancy, restorative capacity, consequence management, continuity of operations (COOP) procedures, training and exercising."[24] These elements echo the *National Strategy to Secure Cyberspace*. Both documents mention the ability to restore attacked systems and continue cyber operations through an attack as key defensive characteristics.

NMS-CO also calls for an in-depth layered defense for continued cyber operations.[25] This layered defense is needed to monitor, detect, report, prevent, and respond to unauthorized access to DoD systems.[26] Such a defense would emphasize the continuation of network operations. Although the document mentions restoring systems elsewhere, its description of a layered defense assumes threats will be mitigated prior to restoring the system.

Although both of these high-level strategy documents deal with cyberspace operations, they differ in their emphasis and the military doctrine attempts to reconcile the differences. The *National Strategy to Secure Cyberspace* centers on defense but "reserves the right to respond [to attacks] in an appropriate manner."[27] The NMS-CO is the military's "comprehensive strategic approach for using cyberspace operations to assure US military strategic superiority in the domain."[28] Doctrine attempts to translate these strategies into specific actions. Joint Publication (JP) 3-13, *Information Operations*, 13 February 2006, provides the military's approach to CNO.

---

[23] Department of Defense, *The National Military Strategy for Cyberspace Operations, December 2006*, 10.
[24] Department of Defense, *The National Military Strategy for Cyberspace Operations, December 2006*, 10.
[25] Department of Defense, *The National Military Strategy for Cyberspace Operations, December 2006*, 14.
[26] Department of Defense, *The National Military Strategy for Cyberspace Operations, December 2006*, 14.
[27] *The National Strategy to Secure Cyberspace, February 2003*, 50.
[28] Department of Defense, *The National Military Strategy for Cyberspace Operations, December 2006*, vii.

JP 3-13, *Information Operations*

JP 3-13 covers a wide range of activities under the heading of information operations (IO). It identifies electronic warfare (EW), CNO, psychological operations, military deception, and operations security as the five core capabilities of IO.[29] Of these five capabilities, this thesis is particularly interested in joint doctrine concerning CNO.

JP 3-13 makes an interesting statement regarding the growth of computing capabilities. "As the capability of computers and the range of their employment broadens, new vulnerabilities and opportunities will continue to develop. This offers both opportunities to attack and exploit an adversary's computer system weaknesses and a requirement to identify and protect our own from similar attack or exploitation."[30] Joint doctrine recognizes the need to balance offensive and defensive computer operations, since both contribute to successful CNO. This doctrinal statement also acknowledges the need for computer defense against the same vulnerabilities the US military may exploit on an adversary's computer system. Doctrine seems to overlook the possibility that adversaries will thwart US attacks with their own defenses or that they might penetrate US defenses as we prepare to attack.

This thesis is also concerned with one of the supporting capabilities listed in JP 3-13, Information assurance (IA). "IA is defined as measures that protect and defend information and information systems by ensuring their availability, integrity, authentication, confidentiality, and nonrepudiation. This includes providing for restoration of information systems by incorporating protection, detection, and reaction capabilities."[31] IA and CND overlap significantly. Joint doctrine chooses to treat IA as a supporting capability rather than

---

[29] Joint Publication (JP) 3-13, *Information Operations*, 13 February 2006, x.
[30] Joint Publication (JP) 3-13, *Information Operations*, 13 February 2006, II-5.
[31] Joint Publication (JP) 3-13, *Information Operations*, 13 February 2006, II-5 - II-6.

incorporating it into CNO, thereby producing an artificial seam in cyberspace defense. Such seams can create opportunities an adversary can exploit, especially when US forces fail to coordinate their efforts across the seams.

Joint doctrine articulates the other four core IO capabilities to a greater extent than it discusses CNO; it refers to classified supplemental guidance concerning the use of CNO.[32] JP 3-13 and the NMS-CO are closely aligned with respect to CNO. Joint doctrine describes using CNA to attack adversary vulnerabilities while using CND to protect friendly information and systems.[33] Unlike the *National Strategy to Secure Cyberspace,* joint doctrine does not focus upon operating through, recovering from, and restoring after a cyber attack on friendly forces.

Joint Publication 3-13 illustrates how strategy is translated into joint doctrine. The Air Force continues this translation into service doctrine and its publications show how it intends to balance CNO between offense and defense. The Air Force is taking a more comprehensive approach to cyber operations than the DoD.

AFDD 2-11, *Cyberspace Operations*

The Air Force views doctrine as "those beliefs, distilled through experience and passed on from one generation of airmen to the next, that guide what we do; it is our codified practices on how best to employ air and space power."[34] According to the Air Force, "doctrine shapes the manner in which the Air Force organizes, trains, equips, and sustains its forces."[35] Doctrine on cyberspace operations illuminates how the service plans to operate in this new domain.

The Air Force is currently coordinating its doctrine for cyberspace operations. The service has drafted Air Force Doctrine Document (AFDD)

---

[32] Joint Publication (JP) 3-13, *Information Operations*, 13 February 2006, II-5.
[33] Joint Publication (JP) 3-13, *Information Operations*, 13 February 2006, II-5.
[34] Air Force Doctrine Document (AFDD) 1, *Air Force Basic Doctrine*, 17 November 2003, 1.
[35] Air Force Doctrine Document (AFDD) 1, *Air Force Basic Doctrine*, 17 November 2003, 3.

2-11, *Cyberspace Operations*, and expects to publish it in the summer of 2009.[36] The document's draft reveals how the Air Force views cyber operations and the balance it is seeking between cyber offense and defense.

Air Force Doctrine Document 2-11 (Draft) maintains a good balance of focus between CNA and CND. The document repeatedly compares cyber and air operations. For example, it defines both freedom of action in the air and in cyberspace as "freedom from attack and freedom to attack."[37] While analogies between the air and cyber domains do not always apply, the comparison does provide a good starting point to comprehend CNO based on Air Force experience in the air domain.

Draft Air Force doctrine defines defensive cyber operations as those that "seek to detect and deny access when intrusions are attempted, determine their sources, minimize the effectiveness of attacks, and help recover in a timely manner."[38] This statement captures the essence of both the *National Strategy to Secure Cyberspace* and the NMS-CO. It covers the detection and subsequent denial of intrusions prevalent in NMS-CO. Its definition of defense also echoes the *National Strategy to Secure Cyberspace* by stressing the importance of minimizing the effects of attacks and restoring systems and capabilities affected by attacks.

Air Force Doctrine Document 2-11 (Draft) categorizes defensive activities as either active or reactive.[39] "Active defenses are the continuous monitoring and analyzing of all activity and identifying anomalous behavior. Reactive defenses are the measures taken to directly counter adversary activities that seek to penetrate a network or actions taken to terminate an ongoing intrusion."[40] The further breakout

---

[36] Lt Col John Gloystein, AETC LeMay Center/DDS, Maxwell AFB, AL, to the author, e-mail, 20 April 2009.
[37] Air Force Doctrine Document (AFDD) 2-11 (Draft), *Cyberspace Operations*, 24 October 2008, 8.
[38] Air Force Doctrine Document (AFDD) 2-11 (Draft), *Cyberspace Operations*, 24 October 2008, 13.
[39] Air Force Doctrine Document (AFDD) 2-11 (Draft), *Cyberspace Operations*, 24 October 2008, 13.
[40] Air Force Doctrine Document (AFDD) 2-11 (Draft), *Cyberspace Operations*, 24 October 2008, 13.

of CND into active and reactive measures reveals that the Air Force has been thinking about how it will defend the cyber domain.

The draft Air Force doctrine strives for a holistic defense in cyberspace that includes protecting physical assets as well as the electromagnetic, logical, and social dimensions of the domain.[41] Figure 1 is taken from the draft AFDD 2-11 and shows the holistic approach the Air Force is taking to defend cyberspace.

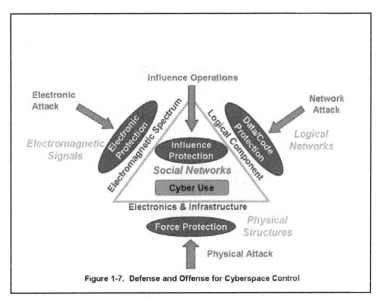

Figure 1-7. Defense and Offense for Cyberspace Control

Figure 1: Holistic Cyberspace Control
Source: Air Force Doctrine Document 2-11 (Draft),
Cyberspace Operations, 24 Oct 08, 15.

Computer security efforts typically focus exclusively on the logical component of network attack and ignore the other dimensions of cyber security. Air Force draft doctrine uses the term Network Defense (NetD)[42] for CND. NetD includes five activities: protection, detection, coordination, survival and recovery.[43] NetD is an in-depth level of defense. "US forces should be capable of operating through a cyberspace attack. They should recognize and isolate an attack while continuing to perform critical actions. Following an attack, they should be able to

---

[41] Air Force Doctrine Document (AFDD) 2-11 (Draft), *Cyberspace Operations*, 24 October 2008, 14.
[42] Air Force Doctrine Document (AFDD) 2-11 (Draft), *Cyberspace Operations*, 24 October 2008, 15.
[43] Air Force Doctrine Document (AFDD) 2-11 (Draft), *Cyberspace Operations*, 24 October 2008, 15.

reconstitute and regenerate capability rapidly."[44] The *National Strategy to Secure Cyberspace* calls for "a national cyber disaster recovery plan"[45] to facilitate the restoration of systems following a cyber attack, but this activity is barely mentioned in the NMS-CO.

The Air Force balances its defensive view of cyberspace with its description of offensive cyber operations. "Offensive operations support US objectives by denying, degrading, disrupting, destroying, altering, or usurping an adversary's ability to use cyberspace."[46] A holistic view of offensive operations mirrors the view of defensive operations as seen in Figure 1. Offensive operations consist of network attack (NetA), attacking the electromagnetic spectrum, and physical attacks on infrastructure.

Air Force draft doctrine defines NetA as the "employment of network-based capabilities to destroy, disrupt, corrupt, or usurp information resident in or transiting through networks."[47] The public and private sectors currently recognize these actions as CNA. As AFDD 2-11 (Draft) points out, "NetA capabilities are entirely dependent on access to the target network. This sometimes requires capabilities specifically designed for the purpose of providing or enabling that access."[48] This statement implicitly assumes that the Air Force can penetrate an adversary's network at will with the right technology. Simultaneously, the Air Force will prevent penetration of its networks by an adversary that likely has access to the same type of technology as the Air Force.

The military has struggled to balance offensive and defensive cyber capabilities as revealed in the postures taken by these documents which

---

[44] Air Force Doctrine Document (AFDD) 2-11 (Draft), *Cyberspace Operations*, 24 October 2008, 23.
[45] *The National Strategy to Secure Cyberspace, February 2003*, 3.
[46] Air Force Doctrine Document (AFDD) 2-11 (Draft), *Cyberspace Operations*, 24 October 2008, 16.
[47] Air Force Doctrine Document (AFDD) 2-11 (Draft), *Cyberspace Operations*, 24 October 2008, 16.
[48] Air Force Doctrine Document (AFDD) 2-11 (Draft), *Cyberspace Operations*, 24 October 2008, 17.

extend from national strategy down to service doctrine. The *National Strategy to Secure Cyberspace* provides a strong defensive stance while the *National Military Strategy for Cyberspace Operations* takes a more offensive stance. JP 3-13 leans slightly more to the offensive side of the equation but remains more defensively focused. AFDD 2-11 (Draft) provides the most balance between offensive and defensive operations. It echoes the *National Strategy to Secure Cyberspace* in calling for a complete defense through the restoration of attacked systems. It also recognizes the difference between physical, logical, and electromagnetic offensive and defensive requirements. This review of strategy and doctrine documents shows that the military is struggling to understand how to defend its cyberspace capabilities, so the next chapter reviews military theory to gain a better understanding of defense.

Chapter 2

A Theory of Defense

Theory then becomes a guide to anyone who wants to learn about war from books; it will light his way, ease his progress, train his judgment, and help him to avoid pitfalls.

Carl von Clausewitz

Where does one look for a theory of defense in cyberspace? The classic military writers described the concept of defense and provided a foundation for defense in general. Carl von Clausewitz is one of the greatest military theorists based on his writings compiled in *On War*.[1] Clausewitz's writings date from the early 1800s, prior to the advent of computers, and focused on land warfare. He provided a descriptive rather than prescriptive theory; his theory described warfare and related issues without prescribing formulas and ways to win war. "Theory exists so that one need not start afresh each time sorting out the material and plowing through it, but will find it ready to hand and in good order. It is meant to educate the mind of the future commander, or, more accurately, to guide him in his self-education, not to accompany him to the battlefield; just as a wise teacher guides and stimulates a young man's intellectual development, but is careful not to lead him by the hand for the rest of his life."[2]

Clausewitz's theory on warfare is descriptive in character. Peter Paret writes that "to devise effective strategic schemes and tactical measures mattered far less to him than to identify the permanent elements of war and come to understand how they function. It is for this

---

[1] Carl von Clausewitz, *On War*, ed. and trans. Michael Howard and Peter Paret (Princeton, NJ: Princeton University Press, 1976).
[2] Carl von Clausewitz, *On War*, 141.

reason that *On War* may still be relevant to issues of war and peace."[3] Clausewitz described the concepts of defense and attack based in the land domain, but these concepts have been applied to other domains of warfare. For example, John Klein applied Clausewitz's theory of defense to the space domain in *Space Warfare.*[4] and these defensive concepts are may also apply to the cyber domain.

Clausewitz began his discussion on defense with two questions and two answers. "What is the concept of defense? The parrying of a blow. What is its characteristic feature? Awaiting the blow."[5] These simple questions and answers hold the key to defense, according to Clausewitz. To parry a blow conveys the idea of first, facing the offensive blow. The defender must meet and then absorb, ward off, or avert the strike of the adversary. The offense initiates the attack and the defender responds from a defensive position.

Clausewitz considers waiting for the offensive blow as the distinguishing feature of defense.[6] This does not mean the defending force remains inactive during the blow. The defenders will prepare to meet the attack with force but wait for the attackers to initiate the action. Offensive actions are part of the defense as the defenders use offensive actions to maintain their position. "So, the defensive form of war is not a simple shield, but a shield made up of well-directed blows."[7]

Preservation, writes Clausewitz, is the object of defense.[8] The defense aims to survive the blow by preserving its forces and holding ground. The defense wants to survive the attack and preserve its strength for a later counterattack. Clausewitz described a defense that

---

[3] Peter Paret, ed., Makers of Modern Strategy: from Machiavelli to the Nuclear Age, (Princeton, NJ: Princeton University Press, 1986), 187.
[4] John J. Klein, Space Warfare: Strategy, Principles and Policy, (New York, NY: Routledge, 2006), 74-78.
[5] Carl von Clausewitz, *On War*, 357.
[6] Carl von Clausewitz, *On War*, 357.
[7] Carl von Clausewitz, *On War*, 357.
[8] Carl von Clausewitz, *On War*, 357.

emerged from the blow strong enough to turn the attack. Clausewitz asserts that "defense is the stronger form of waging war."[9]

In comparing the purposes of defense and attack, Clausewitz states that preservation is the passive purpose of defense and conquest is the positive purpose of attack.[10] "So in order to state the relationship precisely, we must say that *the defensive form of warfare is intrinsically stronger than the offensive.*"[11] [italics in original] After making this statement, Clausewitz points out that defense is stronger but still carries a negative, or passive, object while the offense maintains the positive purpose. Defense "should be used only so long as weakness compels, and be abandoned as soon as we are strong enough to pursue a positive object."[12] This relates back to the object of defense, preservation. The defense must survive the attack with enough capability remaining to mount an offensive.

Defensive warfare is stronger, according to Clausewitz, because of two primary advantages: time and position.[13] "Time which is allowed to pass unused accumulates to the credit of the defender."[14] Time is only an advantage to the defender if it is acted upon. The defense gains nothing from time if it remains idle while the offense prepares for the attack. The defense gains an advantage when it uses the time leading up to an attack to shore up its defenses. Time used to fortify positions, to locate forces on key terrain, and to ensure adequate supplies is time well spent by the defense. Time is of such importance that Clausewitz writes, "it is the nature of all defensive action."[15]

Defense also holds the advantage of position. This is often thought of as the home-field advantage in sporting events. Defense operates on

---

[9] Carl von Clausewitz, *On War*, 359.
[10] Carl von Clausewitz, *On War*, 358.
[11] Carl von Clausewitz, *On War*, 358.
[12] Carl von Clausewitz, *On War*, 358.
[13] Carl von Clausewitz, *On War*, 358.
[14] Carl von Clausewitz, *On War*, 357.
[15] Carl von Clausewitz, *On War*, 357.

their own terrain. They are familiar with it and know its benefits. A defender remains closer to supplies than an attacker. Strong lines of communications can readily provide supplies to the defender. Position also boosts the morale of a defender. The defense fights to preserve its territory, homes, and way of life. Defenders have everything to lose while the attack loses only the opportunity of conquest. These stakes make "it easier to hold ground than take it."[16]

Defense is not an end state envisioned by Clausewitz. "A sudden powerful transition to the offensive—the flashing sword of vengeance—is the greatest moment for the defense."[17] Combatants should only defend until they gain superiority in strength, and then they should "proceed to the active object of the war."[18] Even when defenders do not seek conquest over their attackers, "the fact remains that merely parrying a blow goes against the essential nature of war, which certainly does not consist merely in enduring. Once the defender has gained an important advantage, defense as such has done its work. While he is enjoying this advantage, he must strike back, or he will court destruction. Prudence bids him strike while the iron is hot and use the advantage to prevent a second onslaught."[19]

Defense is a strong position as described by Clausewitz, a notion that runs counter to the natural inclination of many in the military. Attack, not defense, is often seen as the glorious position, but Clausewitz portrays a different image. "Consequently, if we are to conceive of defense as it should be, it is this. All means are prepared to the utmost; the army is fit for war and familiar with it; the general will let the enemy come on, not from confused indecision and fear, but by his own choice, coolly and deliberately; fortresses are undaunted by the prospect of a siege; and finally a stout-hearted populace is no more afraid of the enemy

---

[16] Carl von Clausewitz, *On War*, 357.
[17] Carl von Clausewitz, *On War*, 370.
[18] Carl von Clausewitz, *On War*, 370.
[19] Carl von Clausewitz, *On War*, 370.

than he of it."[20] Strong defenders, confident in the positions they have prepared, await attacks, prepared to unleash "the flashing sword of vengeance"[21] after parrying the initial blows.

Using an example defensive battle, Clausewitz illustrated the strength of the defense. The defender awaited the attack by having chosen "a suitable area and prepared it; which means he has carefully reconnoitered it, erected solid defenses at some of the most important points, established and opened communications, sited his batteries, fortified some villages, selected covered assembly areas, and so forth."[22] The defender has made use of time and position. His defenses will "inflict heavy losses on the enemy at low cost to himself."[23] The defender was confident and secure in his defenses. He has ensured an in-depth defense with reserve forces at all levels.[24] The defender waits until the enemy reveals his plan and uses the majority of his forces before counterattacking.[25] At this point, the defender will use his reserve forces to open "a minor offensive battle of his own, using every element of attack—assault, surprise, and flanking movements. All these pressures will be brought to bear on the battle's center of gravity while the outcome still hangs in the balance, in order to produce a total reversal."[26] The defender will parry the blow, rise from his defensive position with strength, and then switch to the offense against the opposing forces.

Clausewitz described the defensive battle to show the strength of the defense. Defense does not aim "merely to repulse the enemy"[27] but to emerge from the battle strong enough to attack and rout the enemy. "We maintain unequivocally that the form of warfare that we call defense

---

[20] Carl von Clausewitz, *On War*, 371.
[21] Carl von Clausewitz, *On War*, 370.
[22] Carl von Clausewitz, *On War*, 390.
[23] Carl von Clausewitz, *On War*, 390.
[24]Carl von Clausewitz, *On War*, 391.
[25] Carl von Clausewitz, *On War*, 391.
[26] Carl von Clausewitz, *On War*, 391.
[27] Carl von Clausewitz, *On War*, 392.

not only offers greater probability of victory than attack, but that its victories can attain the same proportions and results."[28] Since the defense's underlying purpose can easily be overlooked, Clausewitz repeatedly stressed "what defense is—simply the more effective form of war: a means to win a victory that enables one to take the offensive after superiority has been gained."[29]

While this thesis focuses on defense, an important relationship exists between attack and defense as Clausewitz points out. He described attack as "a constant alternation and combination of attack and defense."[30] The attacker must understand defensive concepts to be effective because "attack itself cannot exist without some measure of defense."[31] Thus, Clausewitz chose to describe the defensive form of warfare before depicting the attack. When Clausewitz described attack, he built on the defensive concepts previously offered and contrasted them to offensive concepts. "It follows that every attack has to take into account the defense that is necessarily inherent in it, in order clearly to understand its disadvantages and to anticipate them."[32]

Applying Clausewitzian Notions of Defense to the Cyber Domain

Clausewitz's theory of defense, based on experience with land warfare, may help us understand how to defend cyberspace. Clausewitzian theory offers insights into the type of defense needed in the cyber domain. His theory provides a solid foundation of thought on which to build a cyberspace defense.

The concept of anticipating and parrying a blow, at the heart of Clausewitz's theory of defense, applies in cyberspace. Cyber security should strive to avert or ward off attacks on information systems. The

---

[28] Carl von Clausewitz, *On War*, 392.
[29] Carl von Clausewitz, *On War*, 370.
[30] Carl von Clausewitz, *On War*, 524.
[31] Carl von Clausewitz, *On War*, 524.
[32] Carl von Clausewitz, *On War*, 525.

Air Force constantly monitors its network against illegitimate activity. As threats are identified, they are acted upon to prevent further damage.

Identifying an attack may be significantly more difficult in the cyber domain than in the land domain. Defenders must identify blows before parrying them. Clausewitz's defender merely had to indentify and anticipate large land forces moving toward an area of operations. Reconnaissance missions provided insight into the direction, capabilities, and intention of the attacking army. Adversaries are not as easy to identify in cyberspace. One person, not an entire army, can penetrate cyber defenses and cause significant damage. Hackers often disguise their activity and portray it as friendly. They may steal friendly users' identities to gain access to the system with malicious intent. Attributing a cyber attack to an individual is also a difficult task. "Attackers can still conceal their point of origin by looping or leap-frogging several computer systems in several countries before finally going into the system that is being attacked as well as those pursuing them."[33] Although it can be harder to detect a cyber enemy, defenders must still prepare to parry their blows in cyberspace just as Clausewitz explained for land warfare.

Awaiting the blow distinguishes defense from attack. Cyber defenders should maintain this mindset. The defense cannot rest on its laurels. Yesterday's defense may have been good enough, but it is insufficient for today's threat. A cyber defense must be dynamic and adapt to the developing technology and tactics used by the adversary. This requires a large effort from the cyber intelligence community. They "must improve the Nation's ability to quickly attribute the source of threatening attacks or actions to enable timely and effective response...these efforts will also seek to develop capabilities to prevent attacks from reaching critical systems and infrastructures."[34] The

---

[33] Arnaud de Borchgrave, "Silent Cyberwar," *Washington Times*, 19 February 2009, http://www.washingtontimes.com/news/2009/feb/19/silent-cyberwar/ (accessed 4 June 2009).
[34] *The National Strategy to Secure Cyberspace, February 2003*, 59.

30

defense developed as the defender waits for the attack must be strong enough to survive the blow and still be able to fight back.

Like their land domain counterparts, cyber defenses should strive for preservation. A land defense too weak to parry the blow will not preserve its forces and will not be strong enough to resist the attacking force. Likewise, "information systems must be able to operate while under attack and have the resilience to restore full operations quickly."[35] A complete cyberspace defense must preserve both the information systems and the data residing on these systems. Cyber defenses must be robust enough to "surviv[e] attacks and ensur[e] mission essential functions remain operational."[36] Detecting an impending attack and waiting to evaluate its consequences is not a defense aiming to preserve cyber forces.

Clausewitz identified time and position as the primary advantages of defense. Time is as important to cyberspace as Clausewitz described it for land forces. Time benefits the cyber defender when it is used to fortify cyberspace defenses. Many cyber attacks succeed because known vulnerabilities have not been repaired. Software developers frequently release product updates, called patches, to repair problems and security gaps as they are identified. These patches only work when they are installed on the system. Defenders who fail to install patches diligently are not fully exploiting their time advantage.

Position is a major advantage of defense described in Clausewitz's theory. Position is also important in cyberspace but in a different way. Although cyberspace is typically considered to be void of geographical features, virtual terrain exists in cyberspace. Firewalls, an example of virtual terrain, fortify positions for the cyber defenders. "A firewall is a program or a device that filters network packets based on rules intended

---

[35] *The National Strategy to Secure Cyberspace, February 2003*, x.

[36] Air Force Doctrine Document (AFDD) 2-11 (Draft), *Cyberspace Operations*, 24 October 2008, 15.

to discriminate between legitimate and unwanted traffic."[37] An attacker must maneuver around or through a firewall in the same manner that an army must maneuver around or through physical barriers.

Cyber defenders can also use position to control access into and out of their network. Routers are network devices that can be programmed to allow or deny different types of network traffic. Their role is analogous to positioning forces at a narrow mountain pass to channelize attacking forces as they approach the defender's territory. Such measures of controlling access only work against known threats; adversaries can still sneak through such access points by masquerading as legitimate traffic.

The cyber domain may have more difficulty exploiting the advantages of position since it is man-made and constantly changing. Cyberspace "is built, not born. Every system and every network can hold its own cyberspace – indeed, it can hold a limitless number of quasi-independent spaces. Cyberspace can appear in multiple, almost infinite, manifestations and forms."[38] Cyber defenders may not be completely aware of the terrain they are charged to defend. A local area network undergoes "terrain" changes when new users and systems are added and removed. Hackers are known to use backdoors into a network. A backdoor is simply an unknown access point into a computer. It can occur when a vulnerability is not patched or could be written into a software program by a malicious programmer.[39]

Both cyber and land domains can be mapped to best position forces to hold the ground. A network map identifies all known systems on a network and can identify users currently logged on to the network.

[37] Ed Bott and Carl Siechert, *Microsoft Windows XP Networking and Security Inside Out: Also Covers Windows 2000* (Redmond, WA: Microsoft Press, 2006), 6.

[38] Martin C. Libicki, *Conquest In Cyberspace: National Security and Information Warfare* (New York, NY: Cambridge University Press, 2007), 5-6.

[39] Fraud Aid Inc, "Backdoors," http://www.fraudaid.com/security_products/articles_information/what_is_a_backdoor.htm (accessed 5 June 2009)

A network map can help identify changes to the cyber domain. New systems and the presence of backdoors can be revealed by comparing a baseline map to a current network map. Larger networks tend to be more complex, making it harder to identify all changes that could reveal vulnerabilities.

A strong cyber defense requires an in-depth, layered approach with reserves held back as described by Clausewitz for land warfare.[40] Each layer of defense would slow down the attacking army, inflicting great losses on the aggressor as it navigated fortified defenses. The reserve forces would be used when the attacking army was weakened and the defense could turn the tide of the battle. The move from the defensive to the offensive would finish off the attacking army.

Multi-layered cyber defenses are created by combining different cyber securities. For example, password-protected log-ins could provide the first layer of protection, software firewalls could provide a second layer, hardware firewalls provide a third layer with network traffic filters as a fourth layer, and the list could continue. Numerous layers of security fortify cyber defenses, but they also impose additional costs.

Reduced efficiency is a cost of multi-layered defense. Each layer of cyber defense can restrict legitimate traffic, making it more difficult for those being defended to take advantage of the domain. This is less of a problem in the physical domain when opposing forces are preparing to attack. People, willing to be inconvenienced when threatened in the physical world, oftentimes complain when inconvenienced in the cyber domain. Cyber defenders cannot expect to alter cyber users' behavior completely to make it easier to defend this domain. The cyber defender must balance a strong defense against the ability of the network users to efficiently perform their functions.

---

[40]Carl von Clausewitz, *On War*, 391.

Reserve cyber forces are another key layer to an in-depth defense. These "forces" in the cyber domain may be additional personnel to monitor the defenses. Data back-ups and system spares also form reserve forces needed in the cyber domain. Current back-ups of network information can help it recover from an attack. Having spare systems pre-configured with the same baseline as the current operating systems provides the second piece of the reserves. "Cyberspace is a replicable construct. Being replicable, it exists in multiple locations at once. Because it is replicable, it is also reparable."[41] This is a distinct advantage of the cyber domain. An attack, virtual or even physical, that destroys a system and the information residing on the system would be countered by connecting the reserve system with back-up data installed. Operations would continue because of the replicable character of cyberspace.

After preparing in-depth cyber defenses, a commander can stand strong and confident in the face of an impending attack. He can "confidently survey the battle as it smolders before his eyes"[42] because he is prepared to hold his territory. This confident commander will wait for his attacker to weaken themselves against his defenses and will then unleash "the flashing sword of vengeance"[43] as he shifts to the offense against his attackers. His reserve forces will ensure that those he defends can continue operations in the most fierce cyber attacks.

[41] Martin C. Libicki, *Conquest In Cyberspace: National Security and Information Warfare*, 5.
[42] Carl von Clausewitz, *On War*, 391.
[43] Carl von Clausewitz, *On War*, 370.

Chapter 3

How Estonia Survived the First Web War

This was the first time that a botnet threatened the national security of an entire nation.

-- Jaak Aaviksoo, Minister of Defense, Estonia

Cyber attacks occur frequently in cyberspace. Individual computer users are susceptible to malicious software such as viruses and spyware. Businesses protect their computer systems against hackers and crackers attempting to steal data such as client information and trade secrets. Government system operators also defend their networks against similar threats. Although each of these sectors has been attacked individually, Estonia survived a widespread, focused cyber attack at the national level that spanned multiple sectors, making it a worthy example for an investigation of marginally effective cyber defenses.

The Underlying Conflict

Estonia shares geographic borders with the Soviet Union but tends to consider itself more Western. It is a small country with a population of 1.340 million.[1] Estonia was occupied by Nazi Germany during World War II and had 7,800 citizens executed by the Nazi's.[2] The Soviet Union controlled Estonia following the war. Estonia strove for independence during the late 1980s. The Soviet Union peacefully recognized Estonia's independence on 6 September 1991.[3] Estonia joined the United Nations

---

[1] US Department of State, "*Estonia*," U.S. Department of State, http://www.state.gov/r/pa/ei/bgn/5377 htm (accessed 8 May 2009).
[2] US Department of State, "*Estonia*," U.S. Department of State, http://www.state.gov/r/pa/ei/bgn/5377 htm (accessed 8 May 2009).
[3] US Department of State, "*Estonia*," U.S. Department of State, http://www.state.gov/r/pa/ei/bgn/5377 htm (accessed 8 May 2009).

on 17 September 1991 and the National Atlantic Treaty Organization (NATO) admitted Estonia as a full member on 29 March 2004.[4]

Estonia is similar to the United States because it possesses strong electronics and telecommunications sectors and is "so wired that it is nicknamed E-stonia."[5] Individuals, businesses, and the government all use cyberspace extensively. "Some 40 percent read a newspaper online daily, more than 90 percent of bank transactions are done over the Internet, and the government has embraced online voting. The country is saturated in free Wi-Fi, cell phones can be used to pay for parking or buy lunch, and Skype is taking over the international phone business from its headquarters on the outskirts of Tallinn."[6]

Political conflict between Russia and Estonia eventually led to the 2007 cyber attack. Soviet leaders placed a bronze statue of a Russian soldier in the middle of Tallinn, the capital of Estonia, in 1947 to symbolize Soviet victory over Germany.[7] This statue became the center of the political conflict, since some Estonians viewed the statue as a reminder of "Soviet occupation and [as] a symbol of oppression"[8] rather than as a symbol of Soviet victory. The Estonian government decided to move the statue to a less prominent location causing debate in the Estonian parliament over the relocation.[9]

A disturbance occurred at the site of the statue on 9 May 2006 between Estonians and ethnic Russians stemming from the symbolism of the statue. To prevent future conflicts, "the police removed a small

---

[4] US Department of State, "*Estonia*," U.S. Department of State, http://www.state.gov/r/pa/ei/bgn/5377 htm (accessed 8 May 2009).

[5] US Department of State, "*Estonia*," U.S. Department of State, http://www.state.gov/r/pa/ei/bgn/5377 htm (accessed 8 May 2009).

[6] Joshua Davis, "Hackers Take Down the Most Wired Country in Europe," *Wired Magazine*, Issue 15.09, http://www.wired.com/politics/security/magazine/15-09/ff_estonia

[7] Swedish Emergency Management Agency, "Sweden's Emergency Preparedness for Internet Attacks," 2008, 9.

[8] Swedish Emergency Management Agency, "Sweden's Emergency Preparedness for Internet Attacks," 2008, 9.

[9] Swedish Emergency Management Agency, "Sweden's Emergency Preparedness for Internet Attacks," 2008, 9.

Estonian group from the Russian-speaking crowd, but it raised the discussion in the Estonian public discourse, as to why the Soviet flags were tolerated and the Estonian one was removed in the middle of the capital of independent Estonia."[10] This event sparked public debate within the Estonian government, which decided to relocate the statue and the graves of several Soviet soldiers from the center of Tallinn in the next year.[11]

The Estonian government began relocating the soldiers' graves on 26 April 2007, and public protests against the move began simultaneously.[12] Within a day small peaceful demonstrations expanded to riots. Estonian officials quickly moved the statue early the next day. This action only made matters worse as "riots led to extensive devastation in central Tallinn, resulting in broken shop windows, plundered shops and fires."[13] Amidst riots and looting, Estonia also found itself under cyber attack on 27 April 2007.

The Cyber Attack

The attack started small and grew in intensity over the next several days. The first strike attempted to deny access to prominent Estonian websites. "Those affected included several political parties, the president's and parliament's websites, the Estonian police, several central authorities and some Estonian legations abroad."[14] The attack quickly expanded to include websites of Estonian newspapers such as the *Postimees*. This newspaper handled a million pageviews on a typical

---

[10] Heiko Paabo, "War of Memories: Explaining 'Memorials War' in Estonia," *Baltic Security & Defence Review* 10, (2008): 14, http://www.bdcol.ee/files/files/documents/Research/1_%20Heiko%20Paabo-War%20of%20Memories-Explaining%20Memorials%20War%20in%20Estonia.pdf.

[11] Swedish Emergency Management Agency, "Sweden's Emergency Preparedness for Internet Attacks," 2008, 9.

[12] Swedish Emergency Management Agency, "Sweden's Emergency Preparedness for Internet Attacks," 2008, 10.

[13] Swedish Emergency Management Agency, "Sweden's Emergency Preparedness for Internet Attacks," 2008, 10.

[14] Swedish Emergency Management Agency, "Sweden's Emergency Preparedness for Internet Attacks," 2008, 11.

day.[15] During the early stages of the cyber attack, "the paper's servers were being swamped with 2.3 million pageviews and had already crashed 20 times."[16] Attackers were trying to overload the *Postimees'* computer systems in an effort to shut them down. The extremely high volume of pageview traffic eventually forced the site to shut down, and it remained down until the paper blocked all international traffic to the site.[17] *Postimees* use of defensive measures kept the site "accessible again within Estonia, but at a cost. Estonia's leading news outlet could not tell the world what was going on in its own country."[18]

According to Joshua Davis, a computer expert reporting for *Wired Magazine,* the attacks consisted of three types of tactics. The first type involved "script kiddies."[19] These independent operators downloaded simple scripts from the Internet and attacked Estonian systems for the thrill of being part of the attack. These scripts, when executed by enough attackers, overwhelm web servers using ping attacks, "a simple request for a response from a web server, repeated hundreds of times per second."[20] Following the attack, Estonia identified the need to increase the "load capacity of public and private sector service servers."[21] Increased capacity would allow the network to handle better this type of threat in the future.

The second type of attack occurred from botnets.[22] Over a million hijacked computers joined the botnet attacks sending data to Estonia systems in a distributed denial of service (DDoS) attack.[23] The targeted systems were flooded by data and eventually forced to shut down. The

---

[15] Joshua Davis, "Hackers Take Down the Most Wired Country in Europe," *Wired Magazine,* Issue 15.09.
[16] Joshua Davis, "Hackers Take Down the Most Wired Country in Europe," *Wired Magazine,* Issue 15.09.
[17] Joshua Davis, "Hackers Take Down the Most Wired Country in Europe," *Wired Magazine,* Issue 15.09.
[18] Joshua Davis, "Hackers Take Down the Most Wired Country in Europe," *Wired Magazine,* Issue 15.09.
[19] Joshua Davis, "Hackers Take Down the Most Wired Country in Europe," *Wired Magazine,* Issue 15.09.
[20] Joshua Davis, "Hackers Take Down the Most Wired Country in Europe," *Wired Magazine,* Issue 15.09.
[21] *Cyber Security Strategy, 2008* (Tallinn, Estonia: Ministry of Defence, 2008), 14.
[22] Joshua Davis, "Hackers Take Down the Most Wired Country in Europe," *Wired Magazine,* Issue 15.09.
[23] Swedish Emergency Management Agency, "Sweden's Emergency Preparedness for Internet Attacks," 2008, 16.

intensity of a botnet attack is proportional to the number of bots involved in the attack.

The final type of attack involved highly sophisticated hackers, according to Davis.[24] These individuals orchestrated the tactics used in the attack. Using a wide range of computer skills, they could "infiltrate individual web sites, delete legitimate content, and post their own messages."[25] The script and botnet attacks used simpler technology to overwhelm Estonian systems with little human oversight needed once these attacks were set into motion. The sophisticated hackers posed a more serious threat because they adapted to the defensive measures the Estonians implemented.

The cyber attacks peaked on 9 May 2007. "Estonian networks were hit every second with an average of four million packets of data."[26] These attacks targeted banks, universities, newspapers and government sites.[27] The attacks forced Hansabank, the largest bank in Estonia, to shut down its on-line services at the peak of the conflict. "The attacks had made it too dangerous to stay connected. The bank shut down all service for an hour and a half and then closed all services to customers outside the Baltic states."[28]

Attacks persisted through the middle of May. "The major botnet attacks stopped as suddenly as they started. The bots appeared to have been set to run for exactly two weeks. After that, the infected computers abandoned the attacks."[29] The targeted systems returned to normal operations after the attacks ceased, but Estonia realized it needed better cyber defenses to cope with any future attacks.

---

[24] Joshua Davis, "Hackers Take Down the Most Wired Country in Europe," *Wired Magazine*, Issue 15.09.
[25] Joshua Davis, "Hackers Take Down the Most Wired Country in Europe," *Wired Magazine*, Issue 15.09.
[26] Rebecca Grant, *Victory In Cyberspace* (Arlington, VA: Air Force Association, 2007), 5, http://www.afa.org/media/reports/victorycyberspace.pdf.
[27] Rebecca Grant, *Victory In Cyberspace*, 5.
[28] Rebecca Grant, *Victory In Cyberspace*, 6.
[29] Joshua Davis, "Hackers Take Down the Most Wired Country in Europe," *Wired Magazine*, Issue 15.09.

Responding to the Attack

As the attacks unfolded, Estonian government and business leaders responded to mitigate the damage. Network administrators, both corporate and government began by filtering network traffic to reduce the loads overwhelming their systems.[30] They tried to filter malicious traffic from legitimate traffic. As previously mentioned, the *Postimees* blocked all outside international traffic to keep its servers running. Filtering kept the systems running, but they could only provide their services to a limited pool of typical users within Estonia.[31]

Network monitoring was beneficial in uncovering the attack. Days into the attack, network monitors in Estonia detected attackers gathering intelligence about their network and attempting to hijack control of their network equipment.[32] As the attacks became increasingly complex, the Estonian government organized a multi-organizational group to coordinate the responses against the attack. The Estonian Computer Emergency Response Team (CERT) was a key member of the team.[33] This team was created to handle all types of computer crises such as a widespread outbreak of a computer virus. The Estonian CERT collaborated and coordinated with similar organizations around the globe to facilitate the "creation of signatures and filtering of traffic close to the sources of the attacks."[34] Collaboration and coordination beyond Estonia was needed since computers outside of its borders were involved

---

[30] Swedish Emergency Management Agency, "Sweden's Emergency Preparedness for Internet Attacks," 2008, 13.
[31] Joshua Davis, "Hackers Take Down the Most Wired Country in Europe," *Wired Magazine*, Issue 15.09.
[32] Swedish Emergency Management Agency, "Sweden's Emergency Preparedness for Internet Attacks," 2008, 13.
[33] Rebecca Grant, *Victory In Cyberspace*, 6.
[34] Swedish Emergency Management Agency, "Sweden's Emergency Preparedness for Internet Attacks," 2008, 14.

in the attack. Foreign organizations helped reduce the effects of the first wave of attacks by "facilitating creation of signatures and filtering of traffic close to the sources of the attacks."[35] The enemy adapted to these defenses in the next wave of attacks. "The number of botnet attacks now increased from jurisdictions without any incident-management organization (CERT) or with a very weak incident management capacity."[36] Attackers, becoming more sophisticated in their methods as defenses adjusted to earlier attacks, displayed their sophistication and the difficulty of defending against such attacks.

Estonians minimized the effects of the attack by blocking the attacks of bot computers. Davis captured the efforts involved in blocking traffic by describing the actions of Kurt Lindqvist, a computer industry expert helping defend Estonia. "Lindqvist sent rapid-fire emails to network operators throughout the world asking for the IP [Internet protocol address] to be blocked at the sources. Their goal was to block traffic before it could enter Estonia's major international connections. One by one, they picked off the bots, and by dawn they had deflected the attackers. Internet traffic into the country hovered just above normal."[37] This time-consuming and exhausting tactic limited the effects of the cyber attacks, but did not completely parry the blow.

The Aftermath

The Estonian cyber attacker's identity has yet to be confirmed. Many attribute the attacks to Russia based on the underlying political conflict concerning the statue and the methods used to carry out the attacks. Russian President Putin considered the Estonian movement of the statue to be a desecration of the memorial.[38] Additionally, the botnet

---

[35] Swedish Emergency Management Agency, "Sweden's Emergency Preparedness for Internet Attacks," 2008, 14.
[36] Swedish Emergency Management Agency, "Sweden's Emergency Preparedness for Internet Attacks," 2008, 15.
[37] Joshua Davis, "Hackers Take Down the Most Wired Country in Europe," *Wired Magazine*, Issue 15.09.
[38] Joshua Davis, "Hackers Take Down the Most Wired Country in Europe," *Wired Magazine*, Issue 15.09.

attacks used against Estonia resembled earlier Russian attacks against political parties that opposed Putin.[39] "Still, the nature of cyber attack made the charges hard to verify. Russia officially denied involvement, and pointed out that, while some Russian Internet accounts were implicated in the attack, Russian computers could have easily been used by hackers outside of Russia itself."[40] The attacking country has yet to claim responsibility for the first cyber war.

Estonia pressed the international community to address cyber issues once the attacks subsided. Estonian government officials sought to establish cyber policies within international organizations. At NATO, they requested that cyber attacks be placed "onto the security-policy agenda by asserting that such attacks should be inserted into NATO's agreement texts on mutual military aid."[41] Estonia's president also spoke to the UN's general assembly and asked the assembly to establish a UN convention on cyber-related issues.[42] The United States' participation in these types of discussions could help create a cyber regime conducive to the defense of cyberspace. "America must be ready to lead global efforts, working with governments and industry alike, to secure cyberspace that is vital to the operation of the world's economy and markets. Global efforts require raising awareness, promoting stronger security standards, and aggressively investigating and prosecuting cybercrime."[43]

The Estonian Ministry of Defence released its *Cyber Security Strategy* in 2008 after some time of reflection on the previous year's cyber attack. Two themes permeated the strategy. First, the strategy stressed the need for global cooperation to make cyberspace more

---

[39] Rebecca Grant, *Victory In Cyberspace*, 7.
[40] Rebecca Grant, *Victory In Cyberspace*, 7.
[41] Swedish Emergency Management Agency, "Sweden's Emergency Preparedness for Internet Attacks," 2008, 18.
[42] Swedish Emergency Management Agency, "Sweden's Emergency Preparedness for Internet Attacks," 2008, 18.
[43] *The National Strategy to Secure Cyberspace, February 2003*, 49.

secure.[44] The second theme was individual users need to be better educated and follow security practices more diligently.[45]

The Estonian strategy contained the lessons it learned and the desired changes to survive future attacks. The strategy opened with five policies for enhancing cyber security:

1. The development and large-scale implementation of a system of security measures.
2. Increasing competence in cyber security.
3. Improvement of the legal framework for supporting cyber security.
4. Bolstering international co-operation.
5. Raising awareness on cyber security.[46]

The second, third, and fourth policies addressed the theme of global cooperation needed to defend oneself against a cyber attack adequately. The first and fifth policies highlight the need for better education and security practices within Estonia.

According to the Estonian strategy, globalization drives the need for international cooperation in cyberspace.

> The global and diffuse nature of cyberspace and of cyber threats means that the potential consequences of attack reach across state borders. It also means, therefore, that ensuring cyber security necessitates close and extensive international co-operation. A global cyber culture—a key component of effective cyber security—can emerge only through a comprehensive co-operative effort involving a wide range of countries, international organizations, private companies and their associations, computer experts, the co-operation networks of law enforcement authorities, academic institutions, non-governmental organisations, etc."[47]

This highlights an opportunity for the United States to shape the cyber regime for the better defense of the cyber domain.

---

[44] *Cyber Security Strategy, 2008* (Tallinn, Estonia: Ministry of Defence, 2008), 3.
[45] *Cyber Security Strategy, 2008* (Tallinn, Estonia: Ministry of Defence, 2008), 3.
[46] *Cyber Security Strategy, 2008* (Tallinn, Estonia: Ministry of Defence, 2008), 3-5.
[47] *Cyber Security Strategy, 2008* (Tallinn, Estonia: Ministry of Defence, 2008), 21.

Estonia is also suggesting changes to international laws concerning cyberspace. "The use of cyberspace is under-regulated in the world."[48] Laws must be addressed on the international level, according to Estonia, because the Internet spans the globe. Their strategy calls for establishing regulations and definitions within international law to secure cyberspace adequately.[49] Expect the United States to become more involved in the discussion of international laws regarding cyberspace. "The United States will actively foster international cooperation in investigating and prosecuting cybercrime. The United States has signed and supports the recently concluded Council of Europe Convention on Cybercrime."[50] President Obama emphasized the need to "protect our prosperity and security in this globalized world" in remarks announcing the new position of Cybersecurity Coordinator.[51]

Estonia's cyber strategy also discussed the need for more cyber-related training and education. The document bluntly stated, "there is insufficient training and preparation in information security."[52] Estonia called for increased funding for universities to provide cyber-related degrees.[53] The nation also tied cyber security to defense-related activities for continued research and development of information systems.[54] In addition to increased education in cyber-related fields, Estonia recognized the need to educate businesses and individuals. "Estonian enterprises, agencies and households have paid less attention to cyber threats and information security and in many senses the level of awareness is insufficient."[55] To address this deficiency, Estonia has created "a public-private sector co-operation project called Data

---

[48] *Cyber Security Strategy, 2008* (Tallinn, Estonia: Ministry of Defence, 2008), 17.
[49] *Cyber Security Strategy, 2008* (Tallinn, Estonia: Ministry of Defence, 2008), 17.
[50] *Cyber Security Strategy, 2008* (Tallinn, Estonia: Ministry of Defence, 2008), 52.
[51] President Barack Obama, "Securing Our Nation's Cyber Infrastructure" (remarks, White House, Washington, DC, 29 May 2009)
[52] *Cyber Security Strategy, 2008* (Tallinn, Estonia: Ministry of Defence, 2008), 16.
[53] *Cyber Security Strategy, 2008* (Tallinn, Estonia: Ministry of Defence, 2008), 16.
[54] *Cyber Security Strategy, 2008* (Tallinn, Estonia: Ministry of Defence, 2008), 16.
[55] *Cyber Security Strategy, 2008* (Tallinn, Estonia: Ministry of Defence, 2008), 15.

Protection 2009...with the aim of developing Estonia into a highly secure information society."[56] Expanding cyber education is also a worthy goal for the Air Force. Fighting in the cyber domain requires expanding education beyond computers and information management to the ability to conceptualize operations in this new war-fighting domain.

Addressing the 2007 cyber attack, Estonia's strategy called for the advancement of three measures to help protect against future attacks. The first measure would impose stricter security requirements upon companies with systems residing on the country's critical infrastructure.[57] Estonia's network is only as strong as the weakest component. One unsecure system can create vulnerabilities for the whole network, so Estonia plans to impose high security standards on any system used in its critical network infrastructure.

The second measure that would help parry a repeat attack would involve increasing the capacity of its infrastructure. According to the strategy, "the availability of the IT infrastructure, including the load capacity of public and private sector service servers, should be increased."[58] Increasing capacity would make it harder for attackers to overwhelm the system. Estonia also addressed the need to monitor and analyze increased network traffic resulting from higher network capacity. As more traffic navigates Estonian networks, network monitors would need improved monitoring and analysis tools to identify cyber threats before they reach their intended targets.[59]

Better cooperation and communication between agencies is the third needed improvement following the 2007 attack.[60] The document described the interaction needed between the public and private sectors. The 2007 attack spanned both sectors and drove the need for open

[56] *Cyber Security Strategy, 2008* (Tallinn, Estonia: Ministry of Defence, 2008), 15.
[57] *Cyber Security Strategy, 2008* (Tallinn, Estonia: Ministry of Defence, 2008), 14.
[58] *Cyber Security Strategy, 2008* (Tallinn, Estonia: Ministry of Defence, 2008), 14.
[59] *Cyber Security Strategy, 2008* (Tallinn, Estonia: Ministry of Defence, 2008), 14.
[60] *Cyber Security Strategy, 2008* (Tallinn, Estonia: Ministry of Defence, 2008), 14.

communication between security experts working in both areas.[61] Interagency cooperation and communication is important for the Air Force's defense of cyberspace. "Situational awareness in cyberspace [is] critical to effective defensive and offensive operations. As in other domains, this is achieved through a combination of means--including joint, interagency and national-level capabilities."[62] The service can focus too strongly on its network with little regard to possible threats originating in other sectors of the network. Communicating with other agencies would provide a stronger defense for the Air Force and other agencies.

The Meaning

The United States should learn from Estonia's experience surviving a cyber war since both countries share several similarities in the area of cyberspace. "The World Bank ranked Estonia's preoccupation with the net as being just behind that of the United States."[63] Estonians and Americans adeptly use the Internet for various services like banking and communications. Both countries are significantly wired with access points distributed around the countries. These similarities mean the Air Force is vulnerable to the same type of threats used in the attacks against Estonia.

The 2007 cyber attack on Estonia displayed the vulnerabilities that come with being a wired nation. The attack did not employ new technologies. Denial of service attacks that flood computer systems are a known tool of hackers, and yet such common malicious tools disrupted the Estonian network. The Estonian defenders had the tools to monitor the network and saw the attack unfold, but could not stop the attacks acting alone.

---

[61] *Cyber Security Strategy, 2008* (Tallinn, Estonia: Ministry of Defence, 2008), 14.
[62] Air Force Doctrine Document (AFDD) 1, *Air Force Basic Doctrine*, 17 November 2003, 17.
[63] Rebecca Grant, *Victory In Cyberspace*, 5.

The Internet spans the globe. Once the Estonians realized that the attacks were coming from all around the world, they knew that the attack required an international response. The tiny Baltic nation relied upon organizations closer to the source of the attack to stop the onslaught of data overwhelming its cyber infrastructure. Coordination and cooperation with these foreign organizations proved vital in slowing down the attack.

The United States should cooperate and communicate with foreign cyber organizations before a cyber attack is launched upon America. "Effort to improve cybersecurity offers the opportunity to rethink how the federal government operates and to build collaboration across organizational boundaries."[64] Estonia recruited allies that could stem the flow of attacks against it because it had previously established relationships with foreign organizations with these capabilities. Developing the rules of engagement regarding actions with other nations before a crisis will save time and effort during an attack. The United States should also strengthen ties between the public and private domains. Any sophisticated cyber attack on the United States is bound to affect both of these cyber domains, necessitating close cooperation across these fronts to parry the attack.

Finally, the attack revealed how important it is to monitor and analyze the network for malicious activity. Estonia monitored its portion of the Internet, filtered traffic, and cut off avenues of attack. This is a much larger task for the United States based on the amount of its traffic but is needed to identify and stop future cyber attacks.

---

[64]James R. Langevin and others. "*Securing Cyberspace for the 44th Presidency*," (Washington, DC: Center for Strategic and International Studies, December 2008), 77.

Conclusions and Recommendations

Train like you fight, and fight like you train.

-- Anonymous

Conclusions

The cyber domain, like other war-fighting domains, requires both attack and defense capabilities. Maintaining capabilities on only the offensive side may leave the Air Force vulnerable to threats on the defensive side. The challenge for the service is to find and maintain the right balance between attack and defense.

United States cyberspace strategies and doctrine reveal conflicting attitudes toward cyber attack and defense. The *National Strategy to Secure Cyberspace* favors a balance towards defense over attack. Attack is an option but the strategy emphasizes defending US activity in cyberspace. The *National Military Strategy for Cyberspace Operations* and Joint Publication 3-13 suggest a balance more suited to attack than defense. Again, both documents discuss attack and defense, but their focus on attack stands out. Air Force Doctrine Document 2-11 (Draft) balances attack and defense evenly.

Air Force doctrine provides a balanced approach to cyber operations, but the Air Force appears to emphasize the offense in its actions. The service was recently in the process of creating a Cyber Command to organize all Air Force cyber operations under a single major command commander. This initiative was overcome by the more pressing need to stand-up Global Strike Command with a focus on the nuclear mission. Cyber operations were subsequently placed under the 24th Numbered Air Force within Space Command.[1]

The reorganization of Air Force cyber forces highlights the emphasis placed on cyber attack capabilities. The *Air Force Cyber Command Strategic Vision*, released in preparation for the stand-up of the command, stressed the offensive character of cyber operations by stating, "Revolutionary technology has presented cyber capabilities, which can provide decisive effects traditionally achieved only through kinetic means."[2] This statement equates cyber capabilities to kinetic attack capabilities. The Air Force's goal as stated in the *Strategic Vision* is the "control [of] cyberspace to deliver sovereign options."[3] The service wants to control the cyber domain and use it to deliver strategic effects like those delivered through strategic bombing.

The Air Force has a history of stressing attack over defense. The Army Air Corps rallied behind strategic bombing in its quest to become an independent service. "General Mitchell's attempts to secure an independent air force in the 1920s was underpinned by his argument that strategic bombing had revolutionized war."[4] The bomber, it was believed, would always get through and win wars by delivering devastating blows to the enemy.[5] "The objective of strategic bombing, whether of a more limited character or not, was to undermine morale in the enemy territory on the one hand and to destroy vital economic targets on the other."[6]

The Army Air Corps was slow to realize that the enemy also possessed the capability to bomb friendly targets. This forced the Army

---

[1] Maj Gen John Maluda, "Communications and Information Transformation" (briefing, Gunter Air Force Base, AL, 2 April 2009).
[2] U.S. Air Force, *Air Force Cyber Command Strategic Vision* (Barksdale AFB, LA: AFCYBER(P), 2008), I.
[3] Air Force, *Air Force Cyber Command Strategic Vision*, II.
[4] Richard J. Overy, The Air War: 1939-1945 (Washington, DC: Potomac Books, 1980), 13.
[5] Richard J. Overy, The Air War: 1939-1945 (Washington, DC: Potomac Books, 1980), 14.
[6] Richard J. Overy, The Air War: 1939-1945 (Washington, DC: Potomac Books, 1980), 13.

Air Corps to create air defenses capable of preventing enemy bombers from getting through. Airpower used offensively could create decisive effects, like those cyberspace is being called to deliver, but the military had to learn to balance its use with defensive capabilities that protected friendly forces.

Cyber operations are not a silver bullet that will win the next war. Like strategic bombing, the offensive capabilities of cyber operations must be balanced with defensive capabilities to prevent the adversary from attacking. The Air Force needs a robust cyber defense in addition to cyber attack capabilities.

Detection and denial are the two key points of the Air Force cyber defense, but detecting and denying are not enough to defend today's cyber environment. The current defense assumes all cyber attacks will be detected and then subsequently denied. This assumption reminds one of early strategic bombing theory.

Strategic bombing theory was built on the assumption that the bomber would always get through. Those advocating offensive bomber operations overlooked the possibility that an adversary could prevent bombers from making it to their targets. The German Air Force, the Luftwaffe, learned this lesson in the Battle of Britain during World War II. Luftwaffe bombers suffered severe losses trying to evade Britain's air defenses. The British designed and implemented an effective air defense that disproved the notion that bombers would always get through to their targets. The British "victory was decisive. Not only had it survived, it ended the battle stronger than it had ever been."[7]

Likewise, Air Force assumptions regarding cyber defense are proving to be false. Recent hacker intrusions into government computer systems have demonstrated the fallacy of detecting all malicious activity in time to prevent intrusions. Most hostile activity is discovered after the

---

[7] Stephen Bungay, *The Most Dangerous Enemy: A History of the Battle of Britain* (London: Aurum Press, 2001), 368.

damage has been done. Only detected attacks can be denied, but there is no guarantee that denial will occur once detected.

The Estonian Web War demonstrated the inability to deny a cyber attack once detected. Estonia detected the attack but was overwhelmed by its strength. The Estonian cyber defenders watched the cyber attack unfold but could not prevent it from continuing. The defenders needed time and the assistance of other nations and international organizations to thwart the attack successfully.

Clausewitz's theory of defense provides concepts applicable to cyberspace. His theory delivered a deeper understanding of defense beyond detection and denial. The goal of Clausewitz' defense was survival, or preservation, of forces. These forces needed to survive to turn on the attacking forces once they had been weakened by the defense.

Detection is an important part of defense. The adversary's actions in cyberspace must be detected before any response can occur. Defensive forces should parry, or deny, the blow once detected. Clausewitz accounts for the importance of detection and denial in defense but moves beyond these two concepts.

Clausewitz described a layered defense as being most effective. Each layer would slow the enemy's advance and weaken the attack. Eventually defending forces would grow stronger than their attackers. At this point, the defending forces would turn the attack and shift to the offense.

Layered defenses would benefit the cyber domain. Multiple layers of defense would slow down a cyber attack, giving defenders time to implement denial efforts or fortify targeted systems. Cyber defenses seek to ensure the survival of systems and data. Multiple layers of defense rather than one or two cyber barriers are needed to ensure survival.

Position is another useful concept in Clausewitz' theory of defense that applies to the cyber domain. Defensive forces, through positioning, uses the terrain and force locations to their advantage. Approaches relying solely on detection and denial do not worry about position because they assume they can repel all attacks, regardless of the position of forces. Positioning in cyberspace can aid the detection of attack by limiting access points. Cyber forces can and should be positioned for the most advantageous defense. Cyber is a virtual environment that permits the creation of "terrain" beneficial to defense and can lead to strong defensive positions.

The active use of time is another benefit of the defense. The defense should use time to strengthen forces and positions. Time allows the defense to become stronger in preparation for future attacks. A defense built on detection and denial can lead to complacency. For example, the notion that all attacks will be detected and denied can cause an organization to ignore further defensive efforts because it assumes every attack will be identified and eliminated before causing damage.

Offense may be needed, but the Air Force must also defend the cyber domain. Defense cannot rely solely on detection and denial. Clausewitz provided clues about robust defenses that can apply to cyber as well as the land domain. Cyberspace is a dynamic environment, and it requires constant vigilance against adversarial activity.

Recommendations

The purpose of this study was to assess the Air Force's ability to survive a cyber attack and continue operations in a contested cyber environment. The service is organizing forces for increased operations in the cyber domain with an increased focus on offensive operations. While cyber attack operations are important, the Air Force cannot focus on the attack at the expense of cyber defense. A balance of both attack and defense should be maintained by the Air Force for successful cyber operations.

Detection and denial are key concepts of cyber defense in the Air Force. They are a good starting point but robust cyber defenses require more. The goal of cyber defense should be the survival of cyber capabilities. Preservation, in a Clausewitzian sense, goes beyond denying attacks. It includes the ability to be attacked and recover as strong after the attack as before. The Air Force should adopt a new mindset for cyberspace defensive operations that focuses upon preservation over denial and counterattack.

The Air Force must maintain situational awareness (SA) over its network and expand SA to other sectors of the domain. This is critical to identify changes that could be the start of malicious activity. The cyber domain spans the entire globe and crosses through public and private sectors. Malicious activity in the private sector could quickly spread into the public networks. SA over all sectors will create a stronger defense and help parry oncoming blows.

The Air Force should increase its defensive position by developing points of contact in the private and public sectors it may need to call when an attack occurs. The day of an attack is too late to call for assistance. Knowing whom to call and developing a working relationship prior to an attack will save time when the cyber bullets start flying. The military is currently only charged to protect the .mil domain, but Estonia identified the need for .gov and .com domains to work together to protect each domain.

The Air Force has many layers of defense in place against cyber attacks, but should explore adding more layers to preserve its threatened cyber capabilities. Common access cards provide the first layer of defense for the network. Firewalls and network filters are examples of additional layers of defense on the Air Force network. A layered defense must balance the need for defense with the need for users to accomplish their mission. There is always risk associated with computers connected to a network and that risk is often less than the productivity that comes

53

with connectivity. Finding the right balance of risk to productivity is an important part of cyber defense. The service should continue to research and develop additional layers of defense that will preserve cyber forces yet appear transparent to users.

The Air Force should use time actively to boost its defensive positions. One of the leading causes for successful cyber attacks is unpatched vulnerabilities. Failure to quickly patch identified anomalies exposes the network to malicious activity. The Air Force has made great advances in this area by creating a service-wide standard desktop. This initiative ensures all computers operate the same software and lets network administrators install patches across the network quickly. The standard desktop creates a common configuration that can be managed at a high level and is advantageous for fixing vulnerabilities across the entire network operating at the same configuration standard. The Air Force should continue to maintain a tight grip on the configuration standards of all computers as a way to rapidly identify and fix vulnerabilities to preserve freedom of action in cyberspace.

The Air Force should ensure cyber reserve forces, data and system spares are adequate and ready for use. Reserve forces are a key part of defense. They ensure continued capabilities during and after an attack. Data back-ups are one example of cyber reserve forces. Regular back-ups provide for continuity of operations should an attack destroy or disrupt the data on a system. If this were to happen, a back-up would restore the data and allow for continued operations. Maintaining spare systems with current configurations could provide rapid recovery in the event of system failure from an attack. The failed system is simply disconnected and a spare system is connected to provide the same capabilities as before. This carries a significant cost. Spare systems are often hard to justify in times of limited resources, but the cost could far outweigh the cost of downtime caused by a system failure with no back-ups.

Incorporating net-out scenarios should be part of Air Force exercises. This is one of the simplest activities to perform in preparation for a cyber attack. Current exercises often include cyber activity that tries to penetrate a network without being detected. This falls short of what should be exercised. The Air Force should hold exercises that "take down" parts of the cyber domain. This will practice the reaction of units affected by the outage. Do they know who to contact? Do they have supplies on hand to continue operations without the cyber domain? What can they continue to do? What can they not do? Exercises involving a net-out environment will force cyber defenders and operators to find answers to these questions quickly, and will prepare the service for such circumstances in times of conflict.

Net-out exercises will also quickly gauge the ability of cyber forces to recover and restore cyber operations. This type of exercise would identify if data back-ups were performed and readily accessible. It would test the availability of system spares and identify those systems requiring back-ups. Net-out exercises would also reveal the second and third order effects that result when that portion of the cyber domain is down. These items are rarely identified until it is too late. If a team plays like it practices, then the Air Force should regularly practice recovering from a cyber attack and restoring its capabilities, so that it is prepared to preserve its forces in a real attack.

America's potential adversaries continually demonstrate the ability to break through our cyber defenses and inflict damage. The Air Force cannot focus exclusively on the offensive side of cyber operations at the expense of cyber defenses. Cyber defense must not stop at detection and denial. It must provide for continued operations through a cyber attack, recovery after an attack, and full restoration of data and capabilities as revealed in the Estonia attack. Implementing these recommendations in the Air Force will provide a more robust cyber defense leading to the preservation of forces and freedom of action in the cyber domain. Preservation should remain the object of defense, even in cyberspace.

Bibliography

Air Force. *Air Force Cyber Command Strategic Vision*. Barksdale AFB, LA: AFCYBER(P), 2008.

Air Force Doctrine Document 1. *Air Force Basic Doctrine*, 17 November 2003.

Air Force Doctrine Document 2-11 (Draft). *Cyberspace Operations*, 24 October 2008.

Air Force Instruction 113-1 AOC V3. *Operational Procedures—Air and Space Operations Center*, 1 August 2005.

Air Force Instruction 33-115 V1. *Network Operations*, 24 May 2006.

Air Force Instruction 33-115 V3. *Air Force Network Operating Instruction*, 15 April 2004.

Air Force Instruction 33-200. *Information Assurance Management*, 23 December 2008.

Air Force Policy Directive 33-2. *Information Assurance Program*, 19 April 2007.

Aljazeera News Service. "Global 'Cyber Spy' Network Revealed," *Aljazerra.net*, 30 March 2009, http://english.aljazeera.net/news/americas/2009/03/200933033 04496652.html.

Borchgrave, Arnaud de "Silent Cyberwar," *Washington Times*, 19 February 2009, http://www.washingtontimes.com/news/2009/feb/19/silent-cyberwar/ (accessed 4 June 2009).

Bott, Ed and Siechert, Carl Siechert. *Microsoft Windows XP Networking and Security Inside Out: Also Covers Windows 2000*, Redmond, WA: Microsoft Press, 2006.

Stephen Bungay. *The Most Dangerous Enemy: A History of the Battle of Britain*, London: Aurum Press, 2001.

Clausewitz, Carl Von. *On War*. Edited and translated by Michael Howard and Peter Paret. Princeton, NJ, Princeton University Press, 1976.

Chilton, General Kevin P. Remarks at the Armed Forces Communications and Electronics Association 2009 Cyberspace Symposium, Omaha, NE., 7 Apr 2009, http://www.stratcom.mil/speeches/23/.

Convertino, Sebastian M. and others. *Flying and Fighting in Cyberspace*. Maxwell Air Force Base, AL, Air University Press, 2007.

Cringley, Robert X. "Parallel Universe," *Technology Review*, January/February 2009, http:// www.technologyreview.com/alt-thinking/hp_feature_article.aspx?id=21806&pg=1.

Davis, Joshua. "Hackers Take Down the Most Wired Country in Europe," *Wired Magazine*, Issue 15.09, http://www.wired.com/politics/security/magazine/15-09/ff_estonia.

Department of Defense. *Annual Report to Congress: Military Power of the People's Republic of China 2009*, Washington, DC: Office of the Secretary of Defense, 2009.

Department of Defense. *The National Military Strategy for Cyberspace Operation, December 2006*, on line at http://www.dod.mil/pubs/foi/ojcs/07-F-2105doc1.pdf. Document is now declassified.

Department of State. *"Estonia,"* U.S. Department of State, http://www.state.gov/r/pa/ei/bgn/5377.htm (accessed 8 May 2009).

Estonia Ministry of Defence. *Cyber Security Strategy, 2008,* Tallinn, Estonia: Ministry of Defence, 2008.

Fraud Aid Inc, "Backdoors," http://www.fraudaid.com/security_products/articles_information/what_is_a_backdoor.htm (accessed 5 June 2009).

Georgia Tech Information Security Center. *Emerging Cyber Threats Report for 2009*, Atlanta, GA: GTISC, 15 October 2008.

Gloystein, Lt Col John, AETC LeMay Center/DDS, Maxwell AFB, AL. To the author. E-mail, 20 April 2009.

Gorman, Siobhan. "Electricity Grid in U.S. Penetrated By Spies," *The Wall Street Journal*, 8 April 2009, http://online.wsj.com/article/SB123914805204099085.html (accessed 12 April 2009).

Grant, Rebecca, *Victory in Cyberspace*, Arlington, VA: Air Force Association, October 2007.

Joint Publication 3-13, *Information Operations*, 13 February 2006.

Klein, John J. *Space Warfare: Strategy, Principles and Policy*, New York, NY: Routledge, 2006.

Langevin, James R. and others. *"Securing Cyberspace for the 44th Presidency,"* Washington, DC: Center for Strategic and International Studies, December 2008.

Libicki, Martin C., *Conquest in Cyberspace: National Security and Information Warfare*, Cambridge, England: Cambridge University Press, 2007.

Lohr, Steve and Markoff, John. "Windows Is So Slow, but Why?," *New York Times*, 27 March 2006, http://www.nytimes.com/2006/03/27/technology/27soft.html?_r=2&pagewanted=all (accessed 12 April 2009).

Maluda, Maj Gen John, Director, Cyberspace Transformation and Strategy. "Communications and Information Transformation." Briefing. Gunter Air Force Base, AL, 2 April 2009.

Markoff, John, "Vast Spy System Loots Computers in 103 Countries,"
    New York Times, 28 March 2009,
    http://www.nytimes.com/2009/03/29/technology/29spy.html?_r
    =1&scp=1&sq=ghost%20net&st=cse (accessed 4 June 2009).

Melinger, Colonel Phillip S., USAF, *10 Propositions Regarding Air Power*,
    Air Force History and Museums Program, 1995.

Obama, Barack, President of the United States. "Securing Our Nation's
    Cyber Infrastructure." Remarks. White House, Washington, DC,
    29 May 2009.

Overy, Richard J., *The Air War: 1939-1945*, Washington, DC: Potomac Books, 1980.

Paabo, Heiko. "War of Memories: Explaining 'Memorials War' in
    Estonia," *Baltic Security & Defence Review* 10, (2008): 14,
    http://www.bdcol.ee/files/files/documents/Research/1_%20Heik
    o%20Paabo-War%20of%20Memories-
    Explaining%20Memorials%20War%20in%20Estonia.pdf.

Paret, Peter, ed., *Makers of Modern Strategy: from Machiavelli to the
    Nuclear Age*, Princeton, NJ: Princeton University Press, 1986.

Richardson, Robert. *2008 CSI Computer Crime & Security Survey*,
    Computer Security Institute, New York, NY: CSI, 2008.

Schiller, Craig A. and others. *Botnets: The Killer Web App.* St. Louis,
    MO, Syngress Publishing, 2007.

Schwartau, Winn. *CyberShock: Surviving Hackers, Phreakers, Identity
    Thieves, Internet Terrorists and Weapons of Mass Disruption*, New
    York, NY: Thunder's Mouth Press, 2000.

Swedish Emergency Management Agency. "Sweden's Emergency
    Preparedness for Internet Attacks," 2008.

US Government Accountability Office. *Cyber Analysis and Warning:
    DHS Faces Challenges in Establishing a Comprehensive National
    Capability*, Washington, DC, July 2008.

US Government Accountability Office. *Information Security: Although
    Progress Reported, Federal Agencies Need to Resolve Significant
    Deficiencies*, Washington, DC, 14 Feb 2008.

US House. *Cybersecurity: A Review of Public and Private Efforts to
    Secure Our Nation's Internet Infrastructure: Hearing before the
    Subcommittee on Information Policy, Census, and National Archives
    of the Committee on Oversight and Government Reform*, 110th
    Cong., 1st sess., October 23, 2007.

US House. *On The United States Strategic Command: Hearing before the
    Strategic Forces Subcommitte of the House Committee on Armed
    Services*, 111th Cong., 17 March 2009.

US White House. *The National Strategy to Secure Cyberspace*, February
    2003.

www.ingramcontent.com/pod-product-compliance
Lightning Source LLC
Chambersburg PA
CBHW060504060326
40689CB00020B/4631